Jeremiah was a young man when God first spoke to him. He was very surprised. It had never happened to him before. It was really quite astonishing.

3

God said, 'I chose you even before you were born, to be a prophet and speak to my people for me. Now it's time for you to begin.'

Jeremiah was very shy.

'I can't possibly be a prophet,' he said, 'I'm too young, and anyway I wouldn't know what to say.'

'Do you think that I will leave you to do the job on your own?' asked God. 'Of course not! I shall give you the words to speak.' And Jeremiah felt a finger touch his lips.

Jere... the great disaster

Story by Penny Frank

Illustrated by Tony Morris

THE LION
STORY BIBLE

25

OXFORD · BATAVIA · SYDNEY

The Bible tells us
how God chose the nation of Israel to
be his special people. He made them a
promise that he would always love
and care for them. But they must
obey him.
This story is about a prophet called
Jeremiah. He really obeyed and
trusted God. He wanted to show God's
people the right way to serve him. But
they did not want to listen.
You can find the story in your own
Bible, in the book called by his name.

Copyright © 1987 Lion Publishing

Published by
Lion Publishing plc
Sandy Lane West, Littlemore, Oxford, England
ISBN 0 85648 750 3
ISBN 0 7459 1770 4 (paperback)
Lion Publishing Corporation
1705 Hubbard Avenue, Batavia, Illinois 60510, USA
ISBN 0 85648 750 3
Albatross Books Pty Ltd
PO Box 320, Sutherland, NSW 2232, Australia
ISBN 0 86760 534 0
ISBN 0 7324 0090 2 (paperback)

First edition 1987, reprinted 1988
Paperback edition 1989

**British Library Cataloguing in
Publication Data**

Frank, Penny
Jeremiah and the great disaster. –
(The Lion Story Bible; 25)
1. Jeremiah – Juvenile literature
I. Title II. Morris, Tony,
1938 Aug 2 –
222'.50924 BS580.J4
ISBN 0-85648-750-3
ISBN 0-7459-1770-4 (paperback)

Printed in Yugoslavia

**Library of Congress Cataloging in
Publication Data**

Frank, Penny.
Jeremiah and the great disaster.
(The Lion Story Bible; 25)
1. Jeremiah (Biblical prophet) –
Juvenile literature. 2. Prophets –
Palestine – Biography – Juvenile
literature. 3. Bible stories, English – O.T.
Jeremiah. [1. Jeremiah (Biblical
prophet) 2. Bible stories – O.T.]
I. Morris, Tony, ill. II. Title. III. Series:
Frank, Penny. Lion Story Bible; 25.
BS580.J4F73 1987 224'.209505
86-15318
ISBN 0-85648-750-3
ISBN 0-7459-1770-4 (paperback)

God told Jeremiah how much he loved
his people. He had loved them from the
very beginning, when he chose Abraham
to start a new nation.

'The trouble is,' God said, 'they so often forget me. They say that they love me and then they go off and worship idols — gods made of stone and wood. Now you are going to be my prophet. You must tell my people to change their ways. Before it is too late.'

7

8

So Jeremiah went out to start his new job. God told him to go to the temple in Jerusalem. If Jeremiah preached there, everyone would hear him.

'God says you must change the way you live,' he told the people. 'God says you do all the things he hates. Then you come to this temple, which is his special place. You have no right to come here unless you change.'

The people listened, but they did not do what God told them to do.

Jeremiah reminded the people of the special promises God had given to Abraham.

'God promised to protect the whole nation if you served him,' he told them.

'You have broken your part of the promise,' Jeremiah said sadly. 'God still loves you, but he can't keep his part of the promise unless you change the way you live.'

The people listened, but still they did not change — as God had told them to do.

So Jeremiah pointed to the potter's workshop, near the temple.

'See the potter?' he asked them. 'If the pot he is making goes the wrong shape, what does he do?'

The people said, 'He squashes it flat and starts again. Everyone knows that.'

'Yes, and that is what God will do, if the nation he is making goes wrong,' said Jeremiah.

The people listened quietly.

God told Jeremiah to buy a large clay jar. Then Jeremiah said to the people, 'God says that because you have disobeyed him he will punish you.'

He lifted the clay jar above his head and then smashed it on the ground.

'This is what God will do to his people,' he said. 'The king of Babylon will come and destroy this city.'

The people looked at the thousands of pieces. Nobody would ever be able to mend it.

The crowd grew angry.

'What right has Jeremiah to pretend to be a prophet?' they said. 'Someone must stop him.'

They did not like being told that they were wrong.

But, although he was frightened, Jeremiah would not stop speaking. He spoke in the temple. He sent messages to the king. In the end, the king sent guards to arrest him.

The king's men took Jeremiah and threw him into a dry well in the palace courtyard. It was deep and slippery. He wouldn't be able to talk to anyone there!

But Jeremiah had a friend in the city. He went to the king and said, 'Your Majesty, it was wrong to throw Jeremiah down the well. Our enemies have surrounded the city. There is no food. Jeremiah will starve and die. Please let me rescue him.'

So Jeremiah was pulled up out of the
well with a rope and kept in prison
instead.

But God meant what he had said. He
was going to punish his people.

One day the enemy broke into the city. They tied up the Israelites with ropes and took them away as slaves to Babylon.

They smashed the houses and burned the palace. God's temple was now just a heap of stones. Only a few people were left in the city — and one of them was Jeremiah.

Jeremiah was very sad, hungry and lonely. He looked around the city which had once been so beautiful. Now it was ugly and empty.

Then he remembered something God had told him.

'The city of Jerusalem will be spoiled and the people taken prisoner. But, when my people have learned to obey me, I promise that I will bring them back home to Jerusalem.'

God still loved his people. There was hope.

The Lion Story Bible is made up of 52 individual stories for young readers, building up an understanding of the Bible as one story — God's story — a story for all time and all people.

The Old Testament section (numbers 1–30) tells the story of a great nation — God's chosen people, the Israelites — and God's love and care for them through good times and bad. The stories are about people who knew and trusted God. From this nation came one special person, Jesus Christ, sent by God to save all people everywhere.

The prophet Jeremiah has a whole Bible book which tells his story and the story of the people of Judah (the last two remaining clans of the old Israelites) in the desperate days before the kingdom fell to the armies of Babylon.

Thanks to a good king, who trusted God, Judah had survived the earlier threat from Assyria (see number 24: *Enemies all around*). But the lesson was soon forgotten. Like the northern kingdom of Israel, the people of Judah refused to listen to God, or to obey him.

God sent Jeremiah to talk them round. But though he tried and tried, no one paid any attention. Jeremiah had a very hard time of it. But, no matter what happened, he knew that God still loved his people and longed for them to come back to him.

The next book in this series, number 26: *King Nebuchadnezzar's golden statue*, tells the famous story of three young men who chose certain death rather than disobey God.